ONLINE
PROFIT STREAMS

21 Proven Ways To Create
Multiple Streams of Profit Online

Disclaimer

This e-book has been written to provide information about Internet marketing. Every effort has been made to make this ebook as complete and accurate as possible. However, there may be mistakes in typography or content. Also, this e-book provides information only up to the publishing date. Therefore, this ebook should be used as a guide - not as the ultimate source.

The purpose of this ebook is to educate. The author and the publisher does not warrant that the information contained in this e-book is fully complete and shall not be responsible for any errors or omissions. The author and publisher shall have neither liability nor responsibility to any person or entity with respect to any loss or damage caused or alleged to be caused directly or indirectly by this e-book.

Contents

INTRODUCTION 5

  1. Freelance Writing 5

  2. Write and Submit 7

  3. Article Marketing 8

  4. Graphic Design 10

  5. Logo and Design Contests 12

  6. Web Design 13

  7. Web Development 14

  8. Create Your Own Information Product – Text 15

  9. Create Your Own Information Product – Audio 17

  10. Create Your Own Information Product – Video 19

  11. Interview and Sell 20

  12. Affiliate Marketing 22

  13. Affiliate Marketing via Videos 23

  14. Sell Others' Products 24

  15. Sell Your Own Product 25

  16. Sell Stock Photos 26

  17. Blogging 28

  18. Blog Management 29

  19. Audio/Video Transcription 30

  20. Video/Audio Editing 31

  21. Odd Jobs 32

Conclusion 33

Bonus Online Profit Streams Methods 34

Resources .... **Error! Bookmark not defined.**

INTRODUCTION

There are many, many ways to make money online, but by no means are they created equal. There are those that don't work out well, there are the scams, and then there are the proven ways to make money online.

In this e-book, we discuss 21 of the best proven ways to make money online. After reading through this, you may very well be fired up to get into making some money online! Note that the order we listed these methods does not imply any greater or lesser value, since people have different strengths and circumstances.

The greatest requirements to make money online are creativity and diligence. The Internet is basically a canvas which you can use to your gain, but you will need to work hard to make things work. With that said, let's begin looking into just how you can make some money online.

1. Freelance Writing

Freelance writing refers to the activity wherein you will write for various clients. The content and length of the material greatly varies. You can find jobs that ask for short 100-word snippets to full-blown thousands-of-words-long e-books. It really depends on what your clients are looking for.

These job requests can be found on many websites dedicated to job requests, and there are even websites specifically catering to writing job requests. A quick Google search for "freelance writing" will pull up a slew of websites.

As a freelance writer, your potential clients are website owners, bloggers, marketers, and small business owners. The subject matter can cover just about anything under the sun – you'll find job requests for rifle scope descriptions to electronic product reviews to skateboarding website copy.

You can choose to focus on a few topics, or go with the flow and take up whatever job requests come your way. The latter tends to be more interesting, even if it can tend to slow down your writing (because of the research required) and lower your output.

One very important facet of this proven way to make money online is keyword research. On the Internet, the search engine is a prime mover because it directs people to where they want to go. Websites are multitudinous and often in competition, and so search engine companies evaluate websites to enable better result filtering and improved user satisfaction. One way that search engines evaluate websites and webpages is by analyzing their keywords for type, frequency, and distribution.

As a freelance writer, your output will often be required to have proper keyword application. You can conduct your own research, or even better, you can get the job order complete with keywords and frequencies. Remember to distribute the keywords as evenly as you can throughout the entire article.

In practice, there are two ways to conduct your freelance writing. One, you can write articles and sell them in batches; think "3 300-word articles on web marketing for x dollars" kind of thing. In this case, you will need to conduct your niche research well, and also know where to go to advertise your output.

The other approach is to get yourself hired by picking up posted requests. This entails more time spent trawling websites for requests and conducting communication with job request owners, but it does provide you with better direction.

Here are some recommended freelance sites:

www.elance.com
www.guru.com

You may also like to try micro outsourcing sites:

www.fiverr.com
www.microworkers.com

2. Write and Submit

This is different from freelance writing because you are not selling your services to a certain person or party. In this proven way to make money online, you write articles on your own time and then submit them to article directories, or even to magazines.

Again, you will see a great range of potential niches and topics. In theory, the range of potential subjects for writing is endless – you're only limited by your expertise and willingness to cover those topics. The length also varies, but in this method you will mostly be limited to articles between 200 words and a thousand words. This is because you are writing "articles" that are readable in one short sitting, and yet are substantial enough to justify the space they occupy.

Article directories are quite simply orderly repositories of written material, generally of the informative sort. A visitor can access the directory and use keywords to search for articles, and then peruse at their leisure. As a writer, these directories allow you to get views for your articles while having a regular outlet for your written material.

How does this make money for you? Well, some directories pay for each visitor who comes to read your articles. Of course, you can also use your articles to market various products and get money from sales or commissions. On the World Wide Web, making money often involves multiple overlapping strategies. This may seem intimidating to the budding Internet-based moneymaker but you'll get the hang of it quickly enough.

Remember to pick out the right categories for your articles, or they could end up getting misclassified and may suffer penalties. Additionally, do not forget your keyword research. Though in this method the keyword research is not as important as in freelance writing, you will still get more hits if you use the right keywords.

3. Article Marketing

What makes article marketing different from the two previous writing-type methods to make money online? It's really a difference in context. Whereas freelance writing means writing and giving your clients partial or full ownership of the material, and writing and submitting means publishing material under your own name for the sake of writing, article marketing is more directly profit-oriented.

Article marketing refers to the set of activities revolving around the writing of articles to promote and sell various products and services. Like in the "write and submit" method, you own your material, but the principle is different. Article marketing is all about making money from your words by selling something that you or someone else is offering.

Though different in spirit, article marketing does also require research into the keywords that are popping and generating lots of interest. Aside from helping you choose a niche, you can also use the keyword variants that get more views, or you could cover the less-used keywords to take advantage of under-explored markets.

These articles are also submitted to various websites and directories where they can get more exposure. More exposure equals more hits equals greater chances of converting into a sale equals more money for you. It's a simple equation, really.

In article marketing, you have to put on your plastic smile and pull out all the stops on your ability to act (as far as writing is concerned). Remember that you are trying to sell something, so the more convincing you are, the more effective and efficient your methodology is. Know your audience and adjust your writing style to get better results.

Recommended article directories to submit to:

www.ezinearticles.com
www.articlecity.com
www.articlebase.com
www.goarticles.com
www.ideamarketers.com
www.articlealley.com

4. Graphic Design

Are you a deft hand at Photoshop or other image editing software? Do you have a good grasp of graphical style and mechanics? Then graphic design may be the path to your online fortune! Graphic design covers a broad range of disciplines that are highly valued in this digital age. To be a great graphic designer, you will need to train yourself to get many skills, and also develop your aesthetic sense and even a personal style.

When we talk about graphic design, we are talking about anything from simple cropping and resizing to editing for clarity and style, all the way to full-blown image creation from scratch. These images make their way into various websites, either as material for use in published articles or as elements in the design of static portions of the website. Some of these images even make their way offline, to printed ads and billboards – that's where the big bucks are! But let's not get too far ahead of ourselves.

More often than not, the images that you will create as a graphic designer will be sued as advertising material by small business owners and web developers. This is not a bad prospect. If you build up a good name for yourself, you can charge more for your work.

Of course, this entails a great amount of creativity, skill, and the ability to translate your clients' wishes into the finished product. However, creative types will find this work fulfilling and enjoyable.

If you want to develop a sense for what's popular, in style, and works well in various contexts, then you should spend lots of time viewing other people's works and analyzing them.

Graphic artists can also work with physical media and translate them into digital forms via scanning or high-definition photography. You can also make a name for yourself as an artist by sharing your work on various art-oriented websites like deviantArt.

If you do share your work as art, be prepared to face both praise and criticism; as they say, beware of the trolls.

If you are going to use images that you did not make yourself, then make sure that you are allowed to do so to avoid lawsuits. Check out royalty-free stock photography options.

Also, brush up on copyright and intellectual property rules so you don't end up "stealing" someone's work, or having the same done to yours.

One trending niche is the creation of backgrounds for personal profile pages like those on Twitter and so on. These backgrounds can also include wallpapers for smartphones and other devices. Take a peek into this method and see if you like it.

The Warrior Forum is a great place to offer your graphic design services to fellow Internet marketers. Go to http://www.warriorforum.com/warriors-hire/ and post your service there. Be sure to include some samples of your work.

5. Logo and Design Contests

There are a surprisingly large number of logo and design contests to be found online. If you are good with image creation using digital or traditional tools, then you will want to keep an eye out for these contests. Each contest is not just a chance to make money – some of the prizes can get quite large – but also to get your name out and in the spotlight.

As with all the highly-creative methods to make money, you will need a goodly bit of imagination and aesthetic sense to pull this off, not to mention the actual technical skills. Many logo contests are held by companies looking to modernize their look, and that means you will need to get a good grasp of the contemporary art styles.

Unlike in graphic design, logo and design contests will constrain you with rules and requirements. However, you can also view these not as restraints but as guideposts to help you direct your energies more efficiently. Remember that your art will face much analysis and criticism, but if you do win, then it was well worth it. You will need to bring your A-game every time, should you choose to pursue this path.

Remember to review the rules and regulations of the contests, specifically with regards to the Intellectual Property rights after submission.

Like the previous method, you can submit your design services at http://www.warriorforum.com/warriors-hire.

6. Web Design

Because first impressions count, all websites need good web design. However, not all websites are created equal. Some are nicer to look at, some are so-so, and others look outdated or just plain yuck.
Web design can pay a lot, but you will need to compete with many strong web designers. This should not be a discouragement, but a challenge that can be overcome!

In web design, you will have to concern yourself greatly with things like layout, color schemes, font faces and more. However, more important than the individual components of design is your ability to deliver a consistent look across all pages of the website.

There has to be a "theme" and also a seamless overall look that binds the whole website together. Even a slight shift in the position of the header or footer can be a jarring and unfavorable experience for the user.

Here are some things you will want to keep in mind: color theory, size and proportion of page elements, readability, bandwidth load, and user-friendliness. It's a lot to keep in mind, but these are all essential for any great website design.

Discussing each of these would take a whole book in itself, so we had best leave them at that.

There's a common joke about how web designers face problems with the translation of the clients' wishes into the design. At most, this is only a half-joke. As a web designer, you will need to have very high quality communication with your client, and we are not talking about the clarity of your webcam and microphone.

You and your client should be able to converse and exchange ideas with each party understanding what's being discussed. Without this communication, you will end up doing many revisions and facing much frustration.

7. Web Development

If web design concerns itself with the appearance of the webpages, web development concerns itself with the underlying structure of the website. To give an analogy, web designers are responsible for the control panel with all the buttons, bells, and whistles, while web developers ensure that all the wires are laid out and attached correctly.

However, that analogy is oversimplifying it. A web developer's world is highly technical, with many different technologies to consider. Aside from knowing these technologies, a web developer also needs to think about how they can be applied and integrated with each other. Compatibility can mean the difference between a few copy-and-pasted program statements and a programming purgatory.

Web developers use various technologies that enable websites to work as they do. Databases, security, bandwidth management, responsiveness, and so many technical criteria keep web developers busy. There is no end to the demand for these services, and if you can deliver high-quality results then you can find yourself rolling in the dough.

Compared to the other proven methods to make money online, web development is the most technical and logical. Programming is not just knowing the code structures and constructs; it is also a mindset. Logic is essential because not only does it enable the programmer to construct the website in an organized and efficient manner, but it also allows succeeding programmers to understand the code easily.

This is one method that you cannot just jump into. It will require training and practice, not to mention self-promotion to get clients. It is not for the faint of heart, but the potential rewards are appropriately great too. Once you get your skills up to par, build a few websites on free hosts so you can have something to show in your portfolio. Also, don't forget to build and trick out your own website, so potential customers can get a feel for what you can do for them.

8. Create Your Own Information Product – Text

A trend that has seen massive growth in the past few years is that of information products. Information products are basically any constructed item containing information that customers may find valuable in one way or another.

The most common type of information product is the electronic book or e-book. When you put your thoughts down on digital paper and package it as a salable product, then you already have an information product.

You can start typing out an e-book using basic word processing software like Microsoft Word or the free alternative called OpenOffice available at www.openoffice.org.

The hardest part of using information products to make money is not the creation, but the marketing. Setting aside the amount of competition you will face, it is not exactly easy to get people to part with their money for things that have no physical form – though in the past couple of years this mindset has been changing. Nevertheless, you will need to put your writing prowess into not just the creation of the product but also in its promotion.

The length of a text information product varies, but normally it is significantly longer than any given "article". That means you are looking at something that is at least a couple thousand words long, written in an organized manner and packaged to be a cohesive unit. That may sound like a task and a half, but experienced writers can do this naturally.

Of course, with any material that gets this long, you will need to consider editing. Editing is the process where someone (preferably not yourself) reviews your work for contiguity, flow, and value per section, aside from the usual spelling and grammatical errors.

If you have friends or family members who don't mind helping you out, then ask them. Don't forget to acknowledge them in your book's public incarnation!

In practice, you can even get others to write your books for you, but you must not forget to read it yourself and edit as needed. It should come out sounding like you, or else you risk being "busted" for using a ghost writer.

Almost any topic is fair game for information products. Even hobbies like gardening and crochet get quite a few books written on them. You should conduct your research to ensure that you have a significant market to eventually sell your product to.

Choose your niche carefully and plan the topics you will discuss so you can sustain the cash flow from your information product series.

Information products are generally informative or instructive in nature, but that is not to say that you cannot sell creative information products. You can produce comics, novels, and other static media works and sell them. A business strategy will be required, but let's leave that for some other day.

On another note, one file format that you may want to look into is PDF. PDF stands for Portable Document Format, and provides improved text flow mechanisms and also greater security – extremely valuable in protecting your intellectual property.

9. Create Your Own Information Product – Audio

Aside from text-based information products, you can also go with audio. Audio is great because it improves the dynamism of your product and encourages customers to pay closer attention to the material. Audio is also a great option for people who want to produce dynamic media while not being confident of their appearances. Audio is "heavier" than text, but it is also more lightweight compared to video (more on this later).

So what can you put into your audio products? Just like with text-based information products, you can cover just about any topic. In fact, audio can deliver more punch than text discussing an identical topic because audio enables you to express emotion more effectively. For example, sarcasm may be hard to detect in written material, but a sarcastic voice and speech pattern reveals many layers of thought and information.

You can conduct your audio recordings as you would your text products. In fact, you can even read out previously-written and published material. It's like getting a second product with only half the effort! Basically, you can make your own audio books. Audio books are great for customers who don't want to bring around clunky e-book readers or fiddle about with tiny smartphone screens, as they can simply transfer the files to their audio players and listen during commutes or whenever they have time.

Another way to conduct your audio recording is as free talk sessions. Instead of reading material, you have a set of topics prepared and you deliver your material like you would when talking with a friend, client, or a hall full of people. You can add some humor to keep things upbeat, or express your emotions and connect with your audience.

You can start recording audio using a program called Audacity, available at http://audacity.sourceforge.net/

You'll want to choose a file format that balances size and quality. MP3 is the most common audio file format, and is a good choice. You don't need the extreme clarity of lossless formats like FLAC, since the files are much larger and you aren't exactly a philharmonic orchestra. You'll probably want to edit out all the dead air and uhms and aahs, as well as adjust the volume. Audacity is a great free program for recording and editing audio, and is a perennial favorite.

Of course, you will want to review and improve your speech. How's your grammar and pronunciation? Do you speak clearly or do you chew up your words? Can you speak spontaneously and expressively? Think, observe, analyze, and improve!

10. Create Your Own Information Product – Video

In the world of information products, video is the heavyweight. It provides the most impact and perceived value. It's also the heaviest in terms of file size or bandwidth. Even the most efficient video file formats still consume more space than the average audio file of the same length. However, file size is a small price to pay for the quality of expression and heightened value that you get.

Just like with audio, you can translate previously published material into video. Of course, you can also cover all-new material, which is definitely of higher value. Unlike text-to-audio conversion, you can't just read out your material. If you are going to convert text to video, then you will need to add illustrations or change the presentation to suit the dynamic potential of video.
No one wants to watch you just reading from a sheet or from the screen – they'd think why didn't you just record it as audio and save us from the excess file size?

Again, just like with audio, you can do a free-talk style of presentation in video. This takes advantage of the dynamic potential of video and allows you to access various "connections" with your audience. If you want to use the emotional connection, you'll want to get your acting chops onboard. You can be serious, or you can be a fool, but don't be a bad actor.

The true value of the video medium comes to the fore when you want to demonstrate a process. As a thought experiment, consider the Japanese art of origami or paper folding. In this case, text with pictures is reasonably effective. Audio is far less effective and efficient – imagine all the times your listeners would go "fold what, where, and how now?" However, if you use a video with voice-over or inserted text, you get maximum instructive capabilities.

Movie editing programs are many and varied, and you are free to explore your options. One great free option for basic video editing is Windows Movie Maker, which comes bundled into some versions of Windows. Check your PC; you may already have it installed.

Recommended screen recording software:

Camtasia – www.techsmith.com
Jing - http://www.techsmith.com/jing.htm
Screenflow (Mac) – www.screenflow.com

11. Interview and Sell

You can make a surprisingly good amount of money from interviewing people and selling the recordings. It all depends, of course, on who you will interview. Interviewing a nobody won't get any hits, no matter how interesting the actual content is – at least, that's how it is at the start.

Why do interviews sell? Maybe it's because people like knowing how other people think. Maybe they want to understand why someone did something. Or maybe there's some drive to uncover more private and intimate details about other people. Whatever the case, interviews can make for some prime salable digital products.

You can generally conduct your interviews in two ways. The first is the traditional Q-and-A format. In this format, you can have questions prepared and then ask them and get answers in return.

While this can be a little dull at times due to lack of spontaneity, it does keep things organized and on track.

The other method to conduct an interview is free talking. In this format, you come up with questions and ask them as they come to mind. This can be a little less organized but more credible because the result comes out as natural and not constructed. Moreover, this leaves you freer to pursue follow-up questions when needed.

If you will use the free talk format, here are a couple of things to keep in mind. One, learn what you can about your interviewee, so you know what avenues of inquiry to pursue. Two, keep a written list of questions on hand, for quick reference when you need to change the topic or simply avoid dead air.

Be sensitive to your interviewee's preferences when it comes to questions. Asking questions that they really don't want to answer can lead to trouble. Your interviewee may clam up, lash out, or simply walk out on your interview. A little sensitivity can go a long way.

As for formats, you can sell text transcripts, audio recordings, or videos of the interview.

12. Affiliate Marketing

Affiliate marketing is an activity where you promote and advertise products or services not as the seller, but as an affiliate. You are not the seller, but you are promoting the product or service. Affiliate marketers get paid by the sellers on a commission basis or on a per-visit basis. For the per-visit basis, it is usually implemented by the seller giving the affiliate marketer a customized link that provides the seller with affiliate marketer data when clicked. This link is then added to one's blog posts or website material, where visitors can see them and click through.

Unlike directly selling to customers, affiliate marketing is easier but can also be rather slow to build up an income flow. On the plus side, you don't need to manage inventory or have space to house the salable products, and you don't need to concern yourself with the sale and shipping systems. On the other side of the balance sheet, you need a lot of visitors to click on your affiliate link – you will need hundreds or thousands of hits to make even a little money.

The trick to affiliate marketing is to get huge amounts of traffic to come to your website. That way, you can let your advertising skills work their magic and get people to click on your affiliate link. There are many methods to increase your website traffic, but the bottom line is that you will need to work to get people to come and visit you.

Many affiliate marketers establish multiple websites to advertise different products or services. This is simply an application of parallelism, and gives you both greater exposure and increased chances of converting visitors into interested parties who will click on your affiliate link. Moreover, you can overcome the bandwidth limitations on a single website by spreading the traffic more evenly; that is at least until you max out the bandwidth on all your sites too! Of course, this multiple-point approach also requires more investments and attention, since all the sites will need traffic boosting.

Clickbank (www.clickbank.com) is the number one affiliate network for digital products. Sign up for free and start promoting products for commission.

13. Affiliate Marketing via Videos

Are you the imaginative type who can make use of video as a medium to express creative and interesting material? Then affiliate marketing via creative videos may be just the ticket. Ever since YouTube took off, there has been a change in the way we look at video as a medium. Now, video is no longer the province of cinematographers, and even the most ordinary person can make a video if they have a camcorder to record it with, and then share via the World Wide Web.

Adding your affiliate links into your videos can be done in several ways. One is as part of the video, such as holding up a board with the URL, or adding a cutaway to display the URL. This is highly recommended, since the viewers have no choice but to see it. Another way is to add the URL via annotations. Yet another way is to add the URL in the description box below your video. For brevity's sake, you may want to use URL shortening services like goo.gl and tinyurl.

Why is video effective in affiliate marketing? Well, it's simply because of the chance that your video will "go viral", or enjoy a massive surge in popularity as people share and link through to your video. With all those hits, you might as well exploit the traffic and turn it to affiliate marketing.

While the traffic tends to come more naturally than it does with marketing blogs, the success of your venture to apply affiliate marketing via video will depend mostly on the content of your video. It must be interesting, compelling, and shareable in order to get the popularity and hits needed to make money from affiliate marketing.

14. Sell Others' Products

The most common form of individual-owned business online is selling products. Just like how your average brick-and-mortar shop gets its products from suppliers and sells them, so to can you buy sellable items at bulk discounts and sell them at a profit via a website. You do not even have to have your own website to sell products online. You can sell via websites like eBay, which even facilitate digital-world "shops". This is traditional buy-and-sell business in a digital context.

The biggest problem is choosing the products that you will sell. There are so many kinds of products out there and so many variants of each type too. You will need to conduct your research to identify which may prove most profitable so you know what and how much to purchase and subsequently sell. You will also want to examine the market to identify what the going prices are so you can maximize profit without offering prices that are too low.

Advertising can play a major role if you have your own website. You need to get people to come to you and browse your offerings, so you need them to know your shop exists in the first place. You can choose to employ banner ads and many other advertising methods. You can even hire affiliate marketers to spread the word for you and pay them on per-visit bases.

You can choose a blog-style website or a full-blown website with multiple pages and linked structure. If you are selling many products, you should know how to categorize them.

As expected of such a business, you will need the physical space to store your inventory, as well as an organized inventory system to keep track of stocks and item locations. You should also explore your options for receiving payment from customers. PayPal is highly recommended, but make sure to provide options for potential customers who don't have PayPal accounts.

15. Sell Your Own Product

Do you have a hobby that produces physical, salable items? Are you good with your hands at making various artisanal craft products? Then why not sell them online?

While it is possible to sell the fruits of your handiwork via a meatspace shop, a cyberspace shop increases your exposure and improves the price point for your products. Just because it seems like no one wants to buy your stuff locally does not mean that there aren't interested parties somewhere in another city, state, or country.

It does not matter if you are making hardcore punk bracelets or cute hats or even paintings, you can sell them online. Etsy is a great digital marketplace for all things handmade. Visit the website and check out just how vibrant the handmade item market is, and how varied the options are.

You can also sell via eBay and other similar websites. Of course, you can also advertise your products on your blog or website, but again you need to somehow increase traffic to improve the likelihood of sales.

There is a chance that your products become so popular that you can turn your hobby into a full-time source of income. When that happens, you will be able to do something that you like and make money out of it. You'd probably want to look for another hobby for relaxation, though.

Avoid skimping on quality. When it comes to handmade objects, people expect attention to detail and care in manufacture, so the implicit standards for handmade products can be quite high. You can actually charge more for a handmade product than a factory-manufactured product, because it is handmade. There is the emotional aspect that subconsciously pushes customers to overlook the extra markup, but only so far.

Since you will be selling your own stuff, you need to think about shipping. This can be tricky if your products are fragile – things like glass sculptures and paintings, for example – and may require special shipping, and consequently special fees. Make sure to factor in shipping costs when taking orders!

16. Sell Stock Photos

With the advent of more affordable high-quality digital cameras, it has become easier than ever to capture scenes from our world. In fact, your photos can be worth quite a bit of money, and we are not talking about entering them in contests – though by all means, you can try.

Stock photography is the production of photographs for paid or even free use. Unlike more traditional photography business models, stock photography does not require the user to pay royalties for each use. The business models applied to stock photography can vary.

The idea is to photograph various objects, scenes, and people in a way that they become symbolic of stereotypes of exemplars of their object type. For example, you can photograph a pickaxe in such a way that it becomes a symbol of hard work, or in a way that it can be used as an element in edited photos.

You can photograph people displaying emotions not for the reason of photographing the person, but for capturing the emotion so the image can symbolize that same emotion, as opposed to portrait photography. Remember to get the consent of the people you photograph!

Stock photographs are valuable commodities. They can make their way into advertisements and even games. The important thing to know is the proper way of assigning rights to your stock photos.

Though some stock photos are free of charge, most are purchased from the sellers. However, stock photos tend to lean towards a "pay once, use unlimited times" model. You can place limits on the time period that the image may be used, or territories where it may be used.

You can also choose to maintain ownership of your photographs or grant exclusive rights to an interested buyer (meaning no one else but the buyer can use the photograph). As with so many things these days, it pays to examine the laws governing the ownership and trade of stock photos.

Recommended stock photo sites:

www.istockphoto.com
www.bigstockphoto.com

17. Blogging

Blogging can make money for you in and of itself, but usually it is best when combined with other techniques such as affiliate marketing and selling your own products.

"Blog" stands for "web log", or an online record of your activities and other things you want to share. Many personal blogs act as public diaries where a blogger can record their emotions and get feedback from the community. There are also marketing blogs, which are constructed solely for the purpose of promoting and selling various products and services.

If you have a personal blog which is intended not for business, but for your feelings and thoughts, then you may want to consider adding a "donation" feature. You might be surprised at the generosity of people who find your blog posts – and even you, by extension – interesting. It won't be much, but it is something.

Of course, the big money in blogging comes from selling products and services. You can use your blog as a canvas for your affiliate links. Depending on the type of blog you are keeping, you will need to balance the business side and the personal, emotional side.

Here's something to remember: privacy on blogs is an illusion. Don't ever think that the stuff you put on your blog (or social networking sites, for that matter) won't be known by undesirable parties. Also, be prepared to face flaming and trolling from the public, as there will always be people who do not know how to express their criticism properly. Ironically, that which was meant to record your emotions and thoughts can become an emotional rollercoaster in itself.

Be careful when sharing personal information on your blog, by which we mean your ID numbers and real-world address. Any chance to become a celebrity also means that there is a chance that you will be targeted by stalkers, thieves, and other ill-wishers.

Recommended blogging platforms:

Wordpress (hosted) – www.wordpress.com
Wordpress (self-hosted) – www.wordpress.org
Blogger – www.blogger.com

18. Blog Management

There's a really popular blogging platform called WordPress. In case you haven't heard of it, it is basically a software program that enables you to write and publish blogs with a lot of the steps being automated. WordPress's functionality is highly flexible and expandable through the use of small bits of code called plugins.

These plugins can perform various tasks automatically, such as monitoring statistics, automatically generating text, and much more. With WordPress and plugins, maintaining a blog is not the problem; choosing and managing your plugins is! There are so many plugins are available, and they are not made equal, not to mention that some are incompatible with each other.

Every problem is a challenge and an opportunity to do business and profit. In this case, you can offer your services as a blog manager, specifically to users in need of help with their plugins. This is a great opportunity, since you can finish your tasks in a few minutes and yet charge disproportionately large amounts of money.

To enable such an opportunity to appear, you need to familiarize yourself with WordPress and its plugins. Moreover, you might want to come up with your "standard" set of plugins and configurations and use it as a template when revamping or tuning a customer's WordPress setup.

You can also offer to perform certain functions for the blog. For example, you can offer to take charge of answering inquiries or managing special orders from customers. This is all about helping blog owners with their problems and getting paid for it.

19. Audio/Video Transcription

It was mentioned previously that you can turn text-based information products into audio or video. However, you can do the exact opposite too. Transcribing the audio and even video scene information can result in a separate salable information product, or an "extra value" add-on.

Transcription can also enable those with damaged auditory senses to experience the media more completely. For example, a deaf person senses loud sounds by the vibrations they cause.

However, in a video, a loud noise can occur and the deaf person won't be able to experience it. However, if the transcript, embedded as subtitles, describes the sound effects, then the deaf viewer may understand the video better.

Aside from transcribing your own material, you can also do the same for others. Offer this service to other people who have their own audio and video information products. Chances are they want transcripts but are not motivated enough to do it themselves.

This is also quite easy as it requires little more than attention to the media being played back and a reasonably good level of typing skill.

20. Video/Audio Editing

Audio and video editing can be time-consuming. Also, the difference between a sloppy edit and something with impact requires a fair amount of skill. If you think you have the skills to pull it off properly, then you can offer audio or video editing services to others.

Lots of people use video editors to arrange, split, join, and enhance videos and audio. However, due to time constraints and a lack of professional focus, the results are often lackluster. That is why more professional editing services can be worth a lot of money.

You can edit anything from interviews to family videos. Think wedding day montage or vacation overview. Even better, you can help others produce more professional-looking ads and potentially-viral videos. It's a question of impact and style.

Choosing a video or audio editing program can be tough. There are so many competing products, and most cost money. It is up to you to do your research and select the ones which you might like working with. Many such editors offer demo versions which, while limited in functionality, can give you a good feel of the features and overall workflow of the software.

Again, if you are going to use sound effects and images that you did not make yourself, you should examine the terms of use for that particular material. No one wants to get sued, right? Look for royalty-free media – though they are not always of high quality, they don't cost much, if at all. On the other hand, there are some royalty-free sound effects or images that can be exactly what you want, so explore and take note of the ones that you like.

21. Odd Jobs

Why focus on just one way to make money online if you can mix it up and keep things fresh by doing odd jobs? Websites like Amazon Mechanical Turk and Fiverr are open marketplaces where people can post and accept job requests with secured and guaranteed channels of payment. On a more professional note, you can join sites like oDesk which get a little more serious and of course, pay off better too.

When we say odd jobs, we mean it in the figurative and literal sense. There are some rather strange job requests to be found online, and it will be up to you and your good judgment to pick the ones that are right for you.

In general though, most jobs are related to the previously mentioned items. You can find request to write articles and reports, requests for video and photo editing, and so on.

Doing odd jobs like this can make it easy to squeeze in a little moneymaking whenever you feel like it. The pay can vary greatly, and you will have to communicate with your potential clients.

However, it does feel more spontaneous and leaves you more capable of adjusting your extra income-making to your daily schedule.

Conclusion

Making money online is not like winning the lottery. It also takes diligence and respect for quality. Just because you won't face your customers directly does not mean you can sacrifice the quality of your work. In the end, producing high quality work can entice more customers and allow you to increase your prices. It's a win-win situation for everyone.

If you are not sure which of these methods you are fit for, why not give them all a try? Many of us have hidden talents that can only be discovered by putting ourselves into situations outside of our normal everyday activities. Who knows, you might very well be the latest self-help guru, ace web designer, art photographer, and so on!

Bonus Online Profit Streams Methods

Bonus Method #1: CPA Marketing

CPA stands for Cost Per Action. In essence, you sign up as an affiliate and promote offers. Whenever someone completes an action, you can earn anywhere from $1-$50, depending on the offer.

Start from www.offervault.com to find hundreds of offers. You need to sign up to a CPA network and get approved first before you're able to promote any offer.

You'll find the highest paying offers are normally anything related to insurance. But you must be aware that it may be a little more difficult to promote insurance offers because there are more steps involved for the prospect to complete.

The easiest CPA offers are those which only require the person to submit his/her email and/or address/zip code, but they normally payout anywhere from $1-$2.

Once you've chosen an offer the next step is to promote. There are various ways of promoting a CPA offer but one proven technique is to use classified ad sites like www.craigslist.com. Submit a classified ad in any country or state, which is highly popular, and don't forget that it must be targeted to the right people.

Be wise and use some of the methods outlined above to promote your CPA offer. There's not just one single method that works. Use your creativity and test what works.

Bonus Method #2: Forum Marketing

Forums are also known as message boards. You can start or reply to threads and the forum members can view and respond to posts.

Most forums nowadays allow a short signature text where you can place a message. We can leverage on this real estate with our website or offer.

The simplest way to is sign up as an affiliate at www.clickbank.com, choose an offer from the marketplace and then changing your forum signature text to include your affiliate link to the offer.

Here's an example signature text:
"Want to learn the 7 secrets to a flat belly? Go here for instant access: [YOUR AFFILIATE LINK]"

You can search for related forums in your niche by simply going to www.big-boards.com, and then joining any or multiple forums.

www.ingramcontent.com/pod-product-compliance
Lightning Source LLC
Chambersburg PA
CBHW070729180526
45167CB00004B/1673